Presented to:

....

By:

....

THE POWER OF

PARTNERSHIP

IN THE CHURCH

JOHN C. MAXWELL
AND TIM ELMORE

Published by J. Countryman, a division of Thomas Nelson, Inc.,
Nashville, Tennessee 37214.

Project editor—Terri Gibbs

Design by Big Picture Design / D² DesignWorks, Sisters, Oregon

ISBN: 08499-5535-1

Published in association with Sealy M Yates, Literary Agent,
Orange County, CA

Printed and bound in the United States of America

FOREWORD

Your job is not an easy one. Leading a church today is more difficult than it has ever been because we live in a society that no longer looks to the church for answers. Yet God established the Church to reach the world. So how *does* a church pastor raise up a dynamic, influential church in our society?

The writer of Ecclesiastes had the answer. He said, "Two are better than one, because they have a good reward for their labor. For if they fall, one will lift up his companion. But woe to him who is alone when he falls, for he has no one to help him up" (4:9–11 NKJV).

The ancient writer gave insight into a pastor's greatest asset in ministry: partnership. It enables you to meet the challenges of ministry with greater strength, tap into more resources, and reap greater victory for the Kingdom of God. I know because I was a pastor. For twenty-six years God gave me the privilege of leading three churches. Each experience was different, but one principle remained the same: PARTNERSHIP MULTIPLIED THE POTENTIAL OF MY MINISTRY.

My passion is to see you realize the same principle in your church. This book is a gift from J. Countryman and The INJOY Group, an organization I founded to partner with pastors and church leaders around the globe to make a difference in the lives of the people they lead. Its pages are filled with true stories of great partnerships—each giving testimony to the incredible value of partnership in the life of any leader.

My prayer is that you will let the warm truths of these stories fill your heart. Learn from them. Grow with them. Share them with your people. Let them give you a taste for the power of partnership. And when

you've turned the last page of this book, ask God how
you can reap the eternal benefits of partnership in your
own ministry.

Your friend and partner in ministry,
JOHN C. MAXWELL
and The INJOY Group

*You can do
what I cannot do.
I can do what you cannot do.
Together,
we can do great things.*

MOTHER TERESA

A Partnership, an Innovation...
and a Lot of Happy People

On a hot summer day, what's the most refreshing treat you can imagine? Ice cream. That's what hits the spot. And that's what people wanted on a hot, sticky day in the summer of 1904. People at the St. Louis World's Fair had walked for hours in the hot sun, and they were ready for something to cool them off. That's why they were lined up for what seemed like miles in front of the booth of Arnold Fornachou to get a taste of his frosty ice cream.

The problem was that Arnold's ice cream was so popular he quickly ran out of paper bowls. The moonlighting teenager scrambled to keep his potential customers by washing and reusing the few ceramic bowls he had on hand. But no matter how hard he worked, many people grew tired of waiting and wandered off in search of another treat. That's when an unlikely partner emerged to save the day.

His name was Ernest Hamwi, a pastry chef who had grown up in Damascus, Syria. In the booth next to Arnold's, he was selling a wafer-thin Persian confection called a *zalabia*. That is . . . he was offering them, but no one was buying them.

When Ernest saw his neighbor's plight, he was struck with a great idea. Grabbing a warm *zalabia*, he twisted it into a cornucopia shape and rolled it in sugar. Then he ran over to Arnold's booth and offered it to him. Still scrambling to wash bowls and wait on customers, Arnold didn't understand what the older man had in mind. But when Ernest handed an ice cream scoop atop a confection cone to a waiting customer, Arnold instantly got the message. A huge smile spread over his face, and in no time, the two men were working side by side—Ernest made "edible bowls," Arnold

scooped ice cream. Back then, they were called World's Fair Cornucopias, and they were the hit of the fair. Today, we simply call them ice cream cones—and they're still a hit.

So the next time you're looking for relief on a hot summer day, think of Ernest and Arnold, and celebrate their partnership by taking a friend out for an ice cream cone.

PARTNERSHIPS SOLVE PROBLEMS—

AND EVERYBODY WINS.

Partnership Passage

You are better off to have a friend than to be all alone, because then you will get more enjoyment out of what you earn. If you fall, your friend can help you up. But if you fall without having a friend nearby, you are really in trouble. If you sleep alone, you won't have anyone to keep you warm on a cold night. Someone might be able to beat up one of you, but not both of you. As the saying goes, "A rope made from three strands of cord is hard to break."

—Ecclesiastes 4:9–12

Partnership Principles

You earn and enjoy more
when you work with a partner.

You recover more quickly from trouble
when you work with a partner.

You experience comfort
when you need it when you work
with a partner.

You are stronger when you work
with a partner.

*It is better to have
one person working with you,
than three
working for you.*

ANONYMOUS

Three Voices—One Heart

In recent years, opera superstars Jose Carreras, Placido Domingo, and Luciano Pavarotti have enjoyed singing together. They've done it frequently, but prior to their first performance the three world-class tenors had never sung together on one stage.

The November 1994 issue of Atlantic Monthly reported that prior to their performance in Los Angeles, a journalist tried to press the issue of competitiveness between the three men. But they quickly disarmed him.

"You have to put all of your concentration into opening your heart to the music," Domingo said. "You can't be rivals when you're together making music."

AN OPEN HEART LEAVES
NO ROOM FOR UNHEALTHY COMPETITION.

What's causing
so much disharmony among
the nations is the fact that some want
to beat the big drum,
few are willing to face the music,
and none want to play
second fiddle.

FORMER SECRETARY OF STATE,
HENRY KISSINGER

Running on the Same Track

During a hike in the woods, a troop of cub scouts came across an abandoned section of railroad track. Each one in turn tried to walk the rail of the track but eventually lost his balance and tumbled off.

Suddenly two boys whispered together and then bet everyone they could both walk the entire length of the track without falling off. Challenged to make good on their boast, the two boys jumped on opposite rails, extended a hand to balance the other—and walked the entire section of track with no difficulty at all.

There in a nutshell is a principle for modern business, community living, and healthy ministry. The day of the contented hermit and successful lone wolf are gone. We do things better, we produce more, and we live better by helping one another. The person who lends a helping hand benefits himself while helping others.

Practicing the power of partnership can make the difference between a good company and a poor one or an effective ministry and an ineffective one.

PARTNERSHIP

MAKES DIFFICULT TASKS EASY.

One Partnership Produces
More Partnerships

Ernest Gordon's book, *Through the Valley of the Kwai*, gives testimony to the amazing effects of one partnership.

Angus McGillivray was a Scottish prisoner in a prison camp filled with American, Australian, and British soldiers—the same soldiers who built the famous Bridge over the River Kwai. During Angus' time there the camp atmosphere had become almost hostile as prisoners stole from each other daily to survive.

To protect their belongings the Scottish prisoners developed a buddy system. Every Scot had a partner known as their "mucker." Angus was given a mucker who was nearing death. In fact, everyone else had given up on him. But Angus did all he could to keep his mucker alive, from surrendering his own blanket to skipping meals each day. Miraculously, his mucker regained health. But shortly thereafter, Angus grew weak and died—a result of starvation and exhaustion.

Word spread about Angus' death and prisoners were moved. They decided to pool their talents for the betterment of the entire camp. One prisoner made violins, another was a carpenter, another a skilled musician, and another a professor. Soon the camp had developed an entire orchestra of hand-made instruments and began a church they called "The Church Without Walls." The services were so compelling, even the Japanese guards attended. Amazingly, in the weeks to come the prisoners also went on to start a university, a library, and a hospital . . . all the result of one partnership.

WHEN ONE PARTNERSHIP LEADS THE WAY,
OTHERS WILL FOLLOW.

PARTNERSHIP MEANS WORK!

It means legwork.

It means teamwork.

It means we work.

Do you recall when Edmund Hillary and his guide, Tenzing Norgay, made their historic climb of Mount Everest? Coming down from the peak Hillary suddenly lost his footing. Norgay held the line taut and kept them both from falling by digging his ax into the ice. Later Horgay refused any special credit for saving Hillary's life. He considered it a routine part of the job. As he put it: "Mountain climbers always help each other."

*One person seeking
glory doesn't accomplish much;
everything we've done
has been the result of people
working together to meet
our common goals.*

RED AUERBACH,
GENERAL MANAGER, BOSTON CELTICS

Partners in Prayer

D r. Wilbur Chapman often tells of the time he went to Philadelphia to become pastor of Wanamaker's Church. After his first sermon, an old gentleman met him in front of the pulpit and said, "You're pretty young to be pastor of this great church. We've always had older pastors. I'm afraid you won't succeed. But you preach the gospel, and I'm going to help you all I can."

"I looked at him," said Dr. Chapman, "and said to myself, 'Here's a crank.'"

But the old gentleman continued. "I'm going to pray that you'll have the Holy Spirit's power upon you, and two others have covenanted to join with me."

Dr. Chapman related the outcome. "I didn't feel so bad when I learned he was going to pray for me. The three became ten, the ten became twenty, the twenty

became fifty, and the fifty became two hundred. They met before every service to pray that the Holy Spirit might come upon me. In another room the eighteen elders knelt so close around me I could put out my hand and touch them on all sides. I always went into my pulpit feeling I would have the anointing in answer to the prayers of 219 men. It was easy to preach . . . a real joy. Anybody could preach with such conditions."

WHEN YOU PARTNER IN PRAYER,
YOU PARTNER WITH GOD.

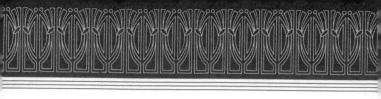

I owe whatever
success I have attained,
by and large,
to my ability to surround
myself with people who are smarter
than I am.

ANDREW CARNEGIE

"There isn't a single person
in the world who can make a pencil,"
stated Newsweek columnist
Milton Friedman as he opened his new
TV series Free to Choose.
"The wood may have come from a forest
in Washington, the graphite from a
mine in South America, and the
eraser from a Malaysian rubber plantation.
Thousands of people cooperate
to make a pencil."

PARTNERSHIP PASSAGE

I promise you that when any two of you on earth agree about something you are praying for, my Father in heaven will do it for you. Whenever two or three of you come together in my name, I am there with you.

MATTHEW 18:18–19

As soon as Peter and John had been set free, they went back and told the others everything that the chief priests and the leaders had said to them. When the rest of the Lord's followers heard this, they prayed together. . . After they had prayed, the meeting place shook. They were all filled with the Holy Spirit and bravely spoke God's message.

ACTS 4.23 24, 31

PARTNERSHIP PRINCIPLES

Partnership moves the hand
and heart of God.

The word *agree* means
to make a harmonious symphony.

There is power in the unity
of God's people. God's presence is
promised when His people work and
pray in partnership.

ACCOMPLISH THE IMPOSSIBLE?

In the latter part of the nineteenth century, when the Methodist church was holding its denominational convention, one leader stood up and shared his vision both for the church and society at large. He told the ministers and evangelists how he believed some day men would fly from place to place instead of merely traveling on horseback. But it was a concept too outlandish for many members of his audience to handle.

One minister, Bishop Wright, stood up and angrily protested. "Heresy!" he shouted. "Flight is reserved for the angels!" He went on to elaborate that if God had intended for man to fly, He would have given him wings. Clearly, the bishop was unable to envision what the speaker was predicting.

When Bishop Wright finished his brief protest, he

gathered up his two sons, Orville and Wilbur, and left the auditorium.

That's right. His sons were Orville and Wilbur Wright. And several years later, on December 17, 1903, those two sons did what their father called impossible. They made four flights that day. The first lasted only 12 seconds, but the fourth lasted 59 seconds and took them 852 feet.

Soon the Wright brothers had built the world's first practical airplane, the Flyer III, and by 1908, the brothers had demonstrated an improved model in France that flew 60 miles in less than two hours.

Two brothers partnered together to accomplish the impossible—and in the process, they changed the world.

WITH PARTNERSHIP AND VISION,
YOU CAN CHANGE THE WORLD.

*God is looking for
[people] through whom He can
do the impossible—
what a pity that we plan
only the things
we can do by ourselves.*

A. W. TOZER

THE BLIND LEADING THE BLIND

You're probably familiar with the biography of Helen Keller. It's the moving story of a deaf and blind girl who would have grown up severely disadvantaged if not for a compassionate woman named Anne Sullivan.

When the two of them met, young Helen was in a cage and would only growl at her new teacher. But Anne, nearly blind herself due to a childhood fever, worked with Helen on every aspect of her life: perception, recognition, personal habits, manners, and speech. In time, the two of them became inseparable partners. By the time Helen reached adulthood, she was a changed woman. She was communicating efficiently, eating by herself, and taking care of her personal needs. Anne Sullivan had brought about an absolute transformation in her protégé, helping her to become an educated, self-sufficient woman.

What you may not know is that Anne Sullivan later experienced her own life crisis. When she suffered a relapse of her previous childhood condition, she became completely blind. Ironically, the "miracle worker" was in need of someone to help her. Can you guess who stepped forward to fill the role? Helen Keller! The recipient of Anne's encouragement and instruction extended her hand to her former mentor. Helen was able to give back to the very one who had given so much to her.

TRUE PARTNERSHIP
MEANS BOTH GIVING AND RECEIVING.

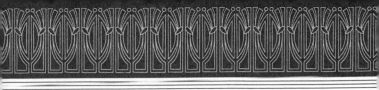

*Partnership is the
ability to work together
toward a common vision.
The ability to direct individual
accomplishment toward organized objectives.
It is the fuel that allows
common people to attain
uncommon results....
Simply put, it is less "me"
and more "we."*

ANONYMOUS

Partnership Passage

So if you consider me a partner, welcome him as you would welcome me. If he has done you any wrong or owes you anything, charge it to me. . . . I will pay it back.

—Philemon 17–19 (NIV)

The Apostle Paul is requesting a favor from his dear friend and partner, Philemon. He is asking Philemon to welcome back a runaway slave—to receive him as a brother. Note the principles we learn about their faith partnership.

Partnership Principles

Faith partnerships
enable us to be vulnerable and take risks.

Faith partnerships
are grounds for asking for deep
commitment.

Faith partnerships
include both giving and receiving.

Friendship + Leadership +
Marksmanship + Workmanship

= Partnership

A Leader for Partnership

He had the cushiest job in the kingdom. Though he was a foreigner, he lived in the palace, spent his days at the court, and tasted wine for the king. And if he'd been content just to hold on to his luxurious position, you wouldn't even know his name, he would never have discovered the incredible power of partnership, and he would have missed the greatest accomplishment of his life.

His name was Nehemiah. Like many Jews of his time, he'd been uprooted from his homeland when Persia conquered Israel centuries before Christ was born. When he learned that Jerusalem was in shambles and Yahweh's name was being ridiculed as a result, he knew he had to do something. After securing permission from King Artaxerxes to return to Jerusalem, Nehemiah set out for the long trip.

Upon arriving at the city, one of the first things he did was inspect the city's walls. As he walked through the rubbish and refuse he became angry. Then his anger turned to passion. Nehemiah determined to rebuild the walls if it was the last thing he did. And that's when it must've hit him. The task was impossible for him to do alone! He needed help—help from others who shared his love of Jerusalem and his passion for God.

So Nehemiah gathered his fellow Hebrews together and laid out a plan for rebuilding the wall. I wonder how they reacted. Did they just stare at him? Or laugh? Jerusalem had been in disrepair for so many years, I doubt any of them even noticed the crumbling wall. But in the end they embraced his vision.

Rebuilding the wall wasn't easy. Neighboring rulers opposed them and conspirators tried to stop them, but the people persevered. They worked side by side, laying stones with one hand and holding a sword in the other.

Remarkably, the wall that had lain in ruins for years was restored in fifty-two days!

It's one of the most remarkable feats recorded in the Bible. And it came about because of the faithfulness of God, the leadership of Nehemiah, and the partnership of the people.

LEADERSHIP HELPS HEARTS
WITH A COMMON PASSION BECOME PARTNERS
FOR A GREATER VISION.

Behind every
able man there are always
other able men.

CHINESE PROVERB

We should not
only use all the brains we have—
but all that we can borrow.

WOODROW WILSON

HOPE FLOATS

One morning in 1878, a young man named Harley decided that the soap and candle company founded by his father ought to produce a new, creamy-white, delicately scented soap. He wanted it to be the best on the market, able to compete with the finest imported Castile soaps of the day.

Harley invited his cousin, James, to help him with the project. James, a chemist, was intrigued by the idea. And since the family's company had been the Union Army's soap supplier during the Civil war, both men felt they had a chance to be successful in the market place. The two men became partners, hoping to create a unique product and earn a good living at the same time.

It didn't take James long to develop the soap formula, and they soon began production. They called their product simply "White Soap," wanting to emphasize its purity. Right away it sold fairly well, but Harley felt that something was still missing. They were somehow missing the product's greatest potential.

They discovered that missing piece as the result of an unexpected contribution from a man named Clem who oversaw the soap vats in their factory. One day Clem left for lunch and forgot to switch off the master mixing machine. He returned to find that too much air had been whipped into the soapy solution. Despite his mistake, he didn't want to discard the batch, so he poured it into hardening and cutting frames and hoped for the best. And that's how history's first air-laden, floating soap bars came to be delivered to stores.

The reaction from customers was overwhelming. The factory was swamped with letters requesting the remarkable soap that bobbed to the surface and couldn't be lost under murky water. When the cousins finally figured out what had happened, they immediately changed

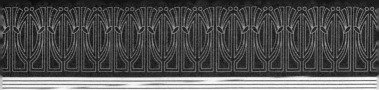

their production method, asking Clem to whip every batch of soap an extra-long time.

They also made one other change. The name "White Soap" seemed far too ordinary for such an innovative soap. As he thought about it one Sunday in church, Harley was inspired by a passage from Psalm 45: "All thy garments smell of myrrh, and aloes, and cassia, out of the ivory palaces...." That was it. They would call the soap "Ivory."

Ivory Soap became the basis of a great partnership between cousins Harley and James—a partnership that continues even to this day. Oh, did I forget to mention their last names? They were Procter and Gamble.

THE BEST PARTNERSHIPS LEAVE ROOM
FOR INNOVATIVE DISCOVERIES.

Partnerships Blend Talent

His name is Elmer Booze. He's a professional page-turner. His job is to follow the score a concert pianist plays and turn pages at the proper times. His goal is to be as unobtrusive as possible, working quickly and quietly without obscuring the pianist's vision. Booze does his job so well that he is called "the ghost."

Though he helps a performer be successful, a good page-turner doesn't share the bows—nor is he listed in the program. If he has done his job right, he remains unnoticed.

Elmer Booze is content in his work because his anonymous contribution adds value to something bigger than himself. Every time he steps on stage, he helps achieve a goal he could never accomplish alone.

PARTNERS PREFER TEAM SUCCESS
TO PERSONAL ACCOLADES.

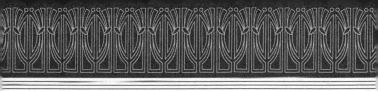

*We have not come
together to compete with one another—
but to complete one another.*

BILL McCARTNEY

FOUNDER OF PROMISE KEEPERS

The Stages of Partnership

1. The Friendship Stage

This is about intimacy. The individuals draw close
relationally—there is *chemistry*.

2. The Formation Stage

This is about identification. The individuals recognize
their uniqueness—there is *contribution*.

3. The Functioning Stage

This is about industry. The individuals begin working
together— there is *cooperation*.

4. The Fruitfulness Stage

This is about innovation. The individuals see results
from the partnership—there is *construction*.

At any point in the process, an additional stage can emerge called The Fragmented Stage. This occurs when any of the individuals violates the relationship or the agreement. This is about infection—and when it happens, at least one party believes there has been a breach of covenant. At this point, there is conflict. All partnerships should work to avoid this stage.

—STEVE MOORE AND TIM ELMORE

WE NEED EACH OTHER

Nobody is a whole team.
Each one is a player. But take away one
player and the game is forfeited.

Nobody is a whole orchestra.
Each one is a musician. But take away one
musician and the symphony is incomplete. . . .

You guessed it.
We need each other. You need someone
and someone needs you. Isolated islands we're not

To make this thing called life work,
we gotta lean and support. And relate and respond.
And give and take.
And confess and forgive. And release and rely. . . .

Since none of us is a whole,

independent, self-sufficient, superb,

capable, all-powerful hotshot—

let's quit acting like we are.

Life's lonely enough without our playing

that silly role.

The game's over. Let's link up.

Charles R. Swindoll
The Finishing Touch

*Few people are successful unless
a lot of other people want them to be.*

CHARLIE BROWER

Fulfillment from a Broken Dream

His life's dream was to be a missionary, and it looked as though it was finally coming true. As the nervous young man sat in the mission agency's office, he assured the interviewer that he and his new bride were committed to working hard, managing their resources as good stewards, and seeing that Christ was shared with as many people as possible. He was confident that everything was coming together for him and his future.

But soon it looked like his dream would fall apart. During their cross-cultural preparation, he and his wife realized she could never endure the rigors of living overseas. She was far too fragile and frail. If they went to Africa as planned, she would certainly die. Confused and emotionally crushed, the young man went to work for his father—a dentist with a small side business that produced unfermented wine for church communion services.

As his father grew older, the young man took over the side business. One day, it struck him that perhaps he could still touch the world for Christ. He could still fulfill the words he had spoken to the mission representative that day. He would work hard, be a good steward of his resources, and see that Christ became known to as many people as possible—he would just do it in a different way. He would keep his promise by financially supporting others who could go overseas as missionaries.

He worked hard and eventually built the company into a huge enterprise. What was his name? Welch Today his grape juice is sold in supermarkets everywhere. And Mr. Welch has given huge sums of money to the cause of world missions. Ironically, he has done far more for world evangelism than he could have by working in the field himself. Because he adapted to his circumstances and blossomed where he was planted, he became a valuable partner in missions around the world.

DON'T PUT LIMITS
ON THE TYPE OF PARTNERSHIP
GOD MAY HAVE IN MIND
FOR YOU.

No Strings Attached

General Eisenhower was a strong leader who understood partnership. When he commanded new subordinates, he taught them a truth about working with people using a simple piece of string. He'd place the string on the table in front of him and say, "Pull it and it'll follow wherever you wish. Push it and it will go nowhere at all."

That's a great lesson for all of us to learn.

YOU CAN DRAW PEOPLE
INTO PARTNERSHIP BUT YOU
CAN'T PUSH THEM.

No One Can Do It All Alone

The Hebrews must have thought Moses could do it all himself. As they traveled across the desert from Egypt to the Promised Land, they followed this amazing man, who came through with miracles from God every time they needed anything. One astonishing miracle followed another: the plagues in Egypt, the parting of the Red Sea, water from a rock, and manna from heaven.

After a while I think the people simply began to expect miracles from Moses. Sure, deep down they knew he was just a man. But somewhere along the way they began to believe that nothing was beyond him. They thought he could do it all himself.

But one day God reminded them of Moses' limitations. It was the day the Amalekites were about to attack the Israeli camp. Moses called upon Joshua, his military leader, asking him to select some warriors. They would go and face the Amalekites and fight, and Moses would climb to the top of a nearby hill to hold up the rod of God in his hands. As long as he had his hands raised, God would grant them victory.

For a while, it worked. Joshua and his small band of warriors were defeating the superior army of their enemy. But after a while, they began to lose. Why? Moses. The man who had led them out of slavery and through the parted Red Sea simply couldn't hold up his hands any longer.

If that had been the end of the story, it would also have been the end of the Hebrews. But two men, Aaron and Hur, climbed up next to Moses, stood on his left and right, and held up his hands until Joshua and his men were completely victorious.

The Hebrews won a war that day and, in the process, they were reminded of a most important principle—even God's anointed leaders need partners to help them accomplish His mighty work.

WHEN WE PARTNER
WITH GOD'S ANOINTED LEADERS,
GOD PARTNERS WITH US.

HUNGRY ANYONE?

Have you ever been to a Thai restaurant? If so, you've probably noticed the unique qualities of Thai food. First, each meal is presented in a beautiful display of colors, shapes, and sizes. Presentation is half the experience.

Second, each meal is a unique blend of foods that are different from what most of us Westerners are used to. Not only are you likely to find noodles, rice, chicken, beef, pork, and a variety of vegetables, but also intriguing taste sensations from chili, several kinds of curries, coconut milk, and lemon grass. Each ingredient is specifically chosen for the distinctive flavor it will add to the dish.

The third characteristic—and the one I find the most intriguing—is the unique *blend* of flavors that creates the Thai taste. The partnership of individual tastes produces a unique effect that can't be duplicated in any other combination.

The same type of thing happens when you partner with people. Something wonderful happens when diverse people work together, something beyond the mere addition of individual contributions. Call it synergy . . . call it collaborative creativity—whatever you call it, it results in a multiplication of talent and potential, not just addition. The unique blend creates a whole new "taste."

HAVE I MADE YOU HUNGRY . . .

FOR PARTNERSHIP?

A SILENT PARTNER

During the 1800s, a famous organist traveled from town to town across America giving concerts. It was in the days of the old pump organs, so in each town he hired a boy to work the pump behind the organ during the concert. After a performance in one town, he couldn't shake the young boy he'd hired.

As the organist walked towards his hotel in the cool of the evening, the boy beamed up at him. "We sure had a great concert tonight, didn't we?"

"You mean I had a great concert tonight," replied the maestro. "You only pumped the organ. Now, go home!"

The next night, the organist gave another concert in the same town, and once again the boy worked the bellows behind the scenes. The opening piece of the concert was a beautiful fugue by Bach. But as the performer masterfully attacked the notes of the second piece, the music suddenly stopped, his rapid fingering bringing nothing more than a faint clicking sound from the keyboard. That's when the little boy stuck his head around the corner of the organ, smiled, and said to the maestro, "We aren't havin' a very good concert tonight, are we?"

A SUCCESSFUL PARTNERSHIP
RECOGNIZES THE IMPORTANCE
OF EVERY PLAYER.

STANDING TOGETHER,
STANDING STRONG

I n April of 1940, German tanks rumbled across the borders of yet another peaceful European country—Denmark. Already possessing control of Austria, Czechoslovakia, and Poland, the powerful Nazi invaders encountered little resistance from the small northern nation.

Soon other countries fell to the Germans as well: Norway, Holland, Belgium, and France—their people bullied, bloodied, and beaten down. As part of their systematic method of intimidation and oppression, the Germans announced that every Dane of Jewish descent would be required to wear a yellow Star of David. They had done the same thing in Germany. Any Jew who failed to comply would be put to death. The Star of David, a proud symbol of their Jewish faith and culture,

would be used to mark them as undesirable members of society—to rob them of their possessions, their dignity, and even their lives.

The Danish government and its people were in no position to do battle against the powerful German army. But their leader, King Christian the Tenth, made a bold move to prevent the Nazis from persecuting the Jewish people among them, one that risked his own life. After the proclamation was made by the occupying army, the Danish monarch called for *all* of his country's citizens to wear the Star of David, for every Danish household to stand as partners with their Jewish neighbors.

What would you have done had you lived in Denmark in 1940? Tremendous fear must have gripped the hearts of those first Gentile citizens to venture from their homes the morning after the king's announcement. Would they be the only ones who had heeded the call? Would they be singled out? Would they be scooped up along with the Jews and executed?

What they saw was nothing short of a miracle. There were Stars of David everywhere. The Jews among them wept when they saw the people's love and support. And because the people stood together, the Nazis' full plan of persecution against the Jews was never carried out in that country.

PARTNERSHIPS OF VALUE ALWAYS
INVOLVE RISK.

That Was a Close Shave

Not long ago, every boy in Mr. Alter's fifth-grade class at Lake Elementary School in Oceanside, California, shaved his head. The event made headlines. Why did they do it? Were they doing it as a protest against a harsh dress code? Was it a publicity stunt to raise funds for the class?

No, they did it for an entirely different reason. The boys got their parents' permission and gladly shaved their heads to make one of their friends feel better. You see, class-mate Ian O'Gorman had developed cancer and was out of school undergoing chemotherapy. All of Ian's hair had fallen out, so to make him feel at home when he came back to class—and so no one would know who the "cancer kid" was—every boy in the class shaved his head. Moved by their unity and spirit, Mr. Alter, their teacher, shaved his, too.

THE ACID TEST OF PARTNERSHIP IS ADVERSITY.

Partnership Passage

Just as iron sharpens iron, friends sharpen the minds of
each other.

—Proverbs 27:17

Partnership Principles

The rough edge of another person
may be the very tool that sharpens us.

Our differences aren't meant to compete—
but to *complete* each other.

We grow more by a positive partnership
than by trying to go it alone.

WHAT IF *You* HELD THE RECORD?

If you know anything about the history of the Olympics, you probably know the name Bob Richards. He is the only man ever to win gold medals in the pole vault in two different Olympic Games. And his feat is a testament to the fact that victories come as the result of both hard work and beneficial partnerships.

Years ago when Bob was trying to break the record for the pole vault held by Cornelius "Dutch" Warmerdam, he kept falling short, no matter what new method he attempted. And it frustrated him. He knew he had the potential to be the best in the world at his sport, but he discovered that there weren't a lot of people who could help him to improve. He was already one of the best in the world, but no matter which coach he talked to, he couldn't find any new insight to help him.

As he wracked his brain, he could think of only one person who had the knowledge to help him—Dutch Warmerdam himself! But how could he ask Dutch to help him break his own record?

As Bob continued training—and saw no significant improvement—that thought lingered in his mind. It seemed so far-fetched, but he could see no other option, not if he was going to improve on his best vault.

Finally, he called Dutch. He decided to be polite but bold.

"Dutch, can you help me?" Bob asked. "I seem to have leveled off. I just can't get any higher."

There was no hesitation. "Sure, Bob," Dutch answered. "Come on up to visit me, and I'll give you all I've got."

Bob was dumbfounded. Here was the greatest pole vaulter in the world—the master—and he was willing to help Bob try to break his own world record.

Bob spent three days with Dutch and, true to his word, the world record holder gave him everything he had. He made corrections to Bob's technique and pointed out things to help him improve. He became Bob's encourager, motivator, and coach. As a result, Bob added an incredible eight inches to his best vault. In the process, he won a gold medal—and set a new world record.

What kind of person willingly helps another to eclipse his accomplishments? A partner.

PARTNERS PUT THE
OTHER PERSON'S SUCCESS AHEAD
OF THEIR OWN.

*Partners must
share vision,
earn trust,
identify gifts,
set goals,
complement weaknesses,
communicate well,
work together,
forgive freely,
finish strong,
benefit mutually.*

Partnership Passage

Just as there are many parts to our bodies, so it is with
Christ's body . . . for we each have a different work to do
. . . each needs all the others.

—Romans 12:4–5 (TLB)

Partnership Principles

None of us are strong in every area.
We need healthy interdependence.

Every part has a niche
and functions to complement the others.

When we work together,
we can actually pull off the work of Christ!

COMMUNITY SERVICE

Have you ever driven through western Pennsylvania? If you have, you're familiar with the Amish community. The people there seem starkly different from the rest of us. They dress differently (dark colors, no buttons), travel differently (horses and buggies—no cars), and even live and eat differently (separate schools, homegrown crops). It's a much simpler life than we're accustomed to.

But many of those differences only touch the surface. To see the more significant ones, you need to see how they interact under pressure. Like what happened the day after a horrifying thunderstorm swept through the countryside one night. The winds were incredible, blowing trees over like straws and flinging everyday objects miles away. Even large buildings were demolished.

When people ventured outside the next morning,

they were shocked to find that the largest barn in the entire Amish community, one that had stood for nearly a century, had been flattened.

But what happened next really shows the heart of the Amish community. People from all over the area converged on the site with lumber, tools, and food. Entire walls were framed and hoisted up by a line of men. And in less than one day, the barn was completely rebuilt—all because of the spirit of partnership that is at the core of the Amish community.

PARTNERSHIP IS AN
ATTITUDE BEFORE IT BECOMES AN ACTION.

Partnerships Share the Responsibility

T hink of autumn. Think of geese flying south for the winter. As each bird flaps its wings, it creates an uplift for the bird immediately behind it. By flying in a V formation, a flock of geese adds at least 72 percent to its flying range compared to each bird flying on its own. That's a great model of synergy—the ability to accomplish more together than apart.

When the lead goose gets tired, he rotates back in the formation and another goose flies point for a while. In doing this they model shared responsibility—leadership that is truly a team effort, not the work of a lone ranger.

As they fly, the geese in the back honk to encourage those up front to keep up their speed and momentum. In doing this they model the power of encouragement and affirmation. Everyone performs better with cheer-leaders around them.

And finally, any time a goose gets sick or is wound-ed and falls out of formation, two geese drop out and follow him down to help and protect him. They stay with him until he is able to fly again or is dead. They then join another formation to catch up with their group. In doing this they model the care that emerges within a group when it works together to reach a com-mon goal.

PARTNERSHIP MULTIPLIES
OUR POTENTIAL AND EXTENDS
OUR REACH.

*Partnerships
don't work for people
unless people work at
partnerships.*

JOHN C. MAXWELL

Holding the Rope

On August 1, 1786, William Carey became an ordained minister. Though just twenty-five years old, a great vision stirred within his soul—a vision he would never have realized without the faithful partnership of a few close friends.

During his first year in ministry, Carey suggested that his Minister's Fraternity send people to Asia to share the gospel. His suggestion was met with harsh rebuke from Mr. Ryland, the chairman.

"Young man, sit down!" he retorted. "You're an enthusiast. When God desires to converse with the heathen—He'll do it without consulting you or me."

Carey was devastated. His colleagues and peers saw his ideas as wildly imaginative, and he was considered a renegade. Everywhere he turned, he met with opposition. But just when he was ready to abandon his vision, he met Thomas Potts, a man who'd been to America and seen the plight of both the Indians and the Africans in the slave trade. He challenged Carey to act on his vision—for the sake of the Indian people.

Carey's enthusiasm was rekindled, but he also began to realize that his dreams would never be fulfilled on his own. In time, God brought other people who offered encouragement and help. One day Carey sat these friends down and showed them how he intended to reach the people of India. He held up a common, everyday rope.

"I will go down to India," he said, "if you will hold the rope." By "holding the rope" he meant praying for him consistently, supporting him financially, and communicating to the churches back in England regularly. They gladly agreed. They would become partners in his vision.

Carey did go to India—and made possible the translation of the Bible into eleven languages. By late 1792 a resolution was adopted creating the first

Protestant mission agency ever. Many have called Carey the father of modern missions, but he viewed his position differently. He called his relationship with the people back home a "brotherhood." He may have been the one to travel to India, but he knew that it was possible only because of the partners back in England who were "holding the rope."

EVEN PARTNERS
WHO REMAIN IN THE BACKGROUND
SHARE IN THE REWARDS.

Nature-Nourished Partnerships

I f you want to see excellent examples of partnership, observe nature. Look at the giant redwoods of California. These trees can tower more than 300 feet in the air. With such height, you might think they require deep roots. Not so. Redwoods actually have very shallow root systems that capture all of the surface moisture possible. Because these roots spread out in every direction, the roots of all the trees are intertwined. As a result, they end up supporting one another and helping each other stand, even in high winds. That is why you rarely see a redwood standing alone. They need one another to survive.

The truth is that most trees growing in a forest help each other in many ways. A Reader's Digest article entitled "What Good is a Tree?" explains that when roots of different trees touch, a fungus develops in the soil that

reduces competition between them. In fact, this substance helps to link the roots of different trees—even of dissimilar species. A whole forest may be linked together. If one tree has access to water, another to nutrients, and a third to sunlight, the trees have a means of sharing with each other.

Someone once said that man is the only real wild animal. Maybe that's because we labor under the notion that we can do everything by ourselves. But if we would just look at the world around us, we would discover that God has woven the need for partnership into the very fabric of the world.

PARTNERS DON'T HOARD RESOURCES—
THEY SHARE THEM.

*None of us
is as smart as all of us.*

Anonymous

When the Going Gets Tough...
the Tough Merge

O n December 1, 1998, the largest corporate
partnership ever was announced from New
York. Exxon and Mobil, the nation's number
one and number two oil giants, agreed to the biggest merger in history. The $73.7 billion marriage created the world's
largest oil company. Both companies, facing cutthroat competition and cut-rate oil prices, decided that it would be
smarter to work together than to work against each other.

They certainly weren't the first large companies to
think that way. Theirs followed the joint ventures of
Citicorp and Travelers, Shell and Texaco, Ameritech and
SBC, GTE and Bell Atlantic, TCI and AT&T, Total and
Petrofina, British Petroleum (BP) and Amoco, Chevron
and Gulf, as well as DuPont and Conoco. But here's the
irony. As in the case of other recent mergers, the Exxon-

Mobil partnership brought together onetime enemies. Fierce competitors, who just months before had stressed their determination to stay independent, they finally conceded that both companies would be better off working in cooperation. Foes became friends, adversaries became allies.

The merger of the two companies also brought about a partnership between the CEOs of Exxon and Mobil, Lee Raymond and Lucio Noto. Raymond has remained chairman of the new organization, and Noto has become its vice-chairman. When asked how he felt about being second in command, Noto noted that this new venture was a partnership.

"I'm going to work for Lee to make this thing work," he said. "I've been with Mobil for 36 years and, believe it or not, for 32 of those years I worked for people," quickly dispelling predictions of conflict.

Corporations in the competitive world of business

are discovering that if they work together they can be more successful. That same lesson is important to Christians. Churches, ministries, and individual believers must learn to work together to reach the world for Christ.

IN A PARTNERSHIP
YOU DO MORE THAN JUST SURVIVE—
YOU THRIVE.

Partnership Passage

Can two people walk together without agreeing to meet?

—Amos 3:3

Partnership Principles

Effective partnerships require mutual goals.

Effective partnerships require a decision
to cooperate up front.

Effective partnerships will not
work without a harmonious relationship.

MAKING MUSIC SIDE BY SIDE

CBS radio newsman Charles Osgood tells the story of a lady named Ruth who lived in a convalescent center. She had been sent there after suffering a debilitating stroke that left her right side incapacitated. Like many stroke victims, she was having a difficult time adjusting to her current condition. Making matters worse was her disappointment at being unable to play the piano, one of her great passions in life.

But then one day the director of the center introduced her to a fellow resident named Margaret. She was also a stroke victim who had been an accomplished pianist. At first Ruth thought the director had brought her and Margaret together to commiserate and console one another. But he had a better idea. You see, Margaret's stroke had affected her left side, just the opposite of Ruth's. So he sat them down side by side at a piano, put a piece of music in front of them, and encouraged them to play it together.

It wasn't easy. At first they struggled, but in time they got better. Before long they were making beautiful music together. As they continued playing together, a beautiful friendship developed between them. And remarkably, as partners they learned to play better together than they ever had on their own.

IN ORDER TO MAKE A MELODY,
PARTNERS MUST FIRST LEARN TO PLAY
IN HARMONY.

A Friend in Need

I t was sheer jealousy that made King Saul want David dead. Young and loyal, David was baffled by his monarch's attitude, and he went into hiding. To survive, he needed an ally. Who did God provide him with? Saul's own son, the man everyone presumed would succeed Saul on the thrown. Jonathan pledged his friendship to David, and even gave him his sword, his armor—and his robe.

Jonathan exhibited all the characteristics of a true friend and dedicated partner. First, he made himself available. He was totally and completely open to whatever action was needed on David's behalf. He said to his friend, "Whatever you say, I will do it for you." His time was David's time.

Second, he was dependable. Out of love he initiated a covenant with David. He had nothing to gain and everything to lose by remaining true to the oath he gave David, but he stuck by it anyway.

Third, he was vulnerable. When he defended David to his father, he risked more than his reputation or even his future position. He risked his very life.

Finally, Jonathan was responsible. Once Jonathan saw how resolute Saul was on killing David, he went to David and warned him to leave—even though he suspected that he would never see best friend again. And he was right. Both Jonathan and his father, Saul, died in war.

David became the next king of Israel, of course. In those days, most monarchs cleaned house by tracking down and killing every one of their predecessor's descendants. David did search for the descendants of Jonathan, and he found one, a crippled man named Mephibosheth. But David treated him like royalty and loved him as if he were his own family. You see, before David and Jonathan parted that last time, they promised to watch after each other's descendants. And David was true to his word. It was the least he could do for his loyal friend, the best partner anyone could ever have.

THE LOYALTY

OF GREAT PARTNERSHIPS LIVES

BEYOND US.

We are made for cooperation,
like feet, like hands, like eyelids,
like the rows of the upper and lower teeth.
To act against one another
then is contrary to nature,
and it is acting against one another
to be vexed and turn away.

MARCUS AURELIUS

Partnership Passage

Now I tell you to love each other, as I have loved you. The greatest way to show love for friends is to die for them. And you are my friends, if you obey me. Servants don't know what their master is doing, and so I don't speak to you as my servants. I speak to you as my friends, and I have told you everything that my Father has told me.

—JOHN 15:12–15

Partnership Principles

Love is the highest law in partnership.

We communicate love by committing our life to our partnerships.

Mutual service is the mark of true partnership.

Complete honesty and trust is the acid test of a healthy partnership.

It is raining still. . . .
Maybe it is not one of those showers that
is here one minute and gone the next,
as I had so boldly assumed.
Maybe none of them are. After all,
life in itself is a chain of rainy days.
But there are times when not all of us have
umbrellas to walk under.
Those are the times when we need people
who are willing to lend their umbrellas
to a wet stranger on a rainy day.
I think I'll go for a walk
with my umbrella.

SUN-YOUNG PARK

Only Death Can Part Us Now

David Livingstone was a talented doctor, missionary, and adventurous explorer. What you may not know is that he was a sickly man. When he ventured into Africa in the nineteenth century, he took a goat with him because he needed goat's milk for health reasons.

As he explored the interior of the African continent, Livingstone's greatest desire was to reach African tribes with the message of Christ. But to do that, he would have to overcome some incredible barriers: differences in race, culture, and language. Few of the people trusted him. The task looked impossible.

But then one day a tribesman gave him some advice that provided the breakthrough he needed. "You need to cut a covenant," he said.

"What do you mean by that?" asked Livingstone.

The man explained that when two parties—even two warring parties—cut a covenant, they immediately became involved in a cooperative relationship. Everything that one party possessed then belonged to the other. A covenant was serious. It was sealed with blood and was binding until death.

Livingstone got excited about the possibility of progress in his missionary work. But as he was preparing to cut a covenant with one of the tribes it struck him— he would have to give up his goat! It would no longer belong to him, but to the tribe, and without that animal, he would face certain death.

It was a terrible decision to have to make, but he decided to go through with it, even if it meant a slow death for him. He believed it might be the best opportunity for Africans of that generation to hear the gospel and accept Jesus as Savior.

Little did he know how wise that decision would be.

In the days that followed, David Livingstone began to understand just how powerful a covenant partnerships could be. Not only did he live, he had access to everything the tribe had—including his goat. Both parties shared everything. But even greater was his discovery that a covenant with one tribe gave him access to other tribes as well. Suddenly, he was no longer an outsider. He was part of huge family of tribes all linked together by covenants.

PARTNER ONCE,
AND IT OPENS THE DOOR FOR
OTHER PARTNERSHIPS.

Hanging By a Thread

On November 20, 1988, the *Los Angeles Times* reported the following story:

A screaming woman trapped in a car dangling from a freeway transition road in East Los Angeles was rescued Saturday morning. The nineteen-year-old woman apparently fell asleep behind the wheel about 12:15 a.m. The car plunged through a guardrail and was left dangling by its left rear wheel. A half dozen passing motorists stopped, grabbed some ropes from one of their vehicles, tied the ropes to the back of the woman's car, and hung on until fire units arrived. A ladder was extended from below to help stabilize the car while firefighters tied the vehicle to tow trucks with cables and chains. It was quite an ordeal.

"Every time we would move the car," said one of

the rescuers, "she would yell and scream. She was in terrible pain."

It took almost two and a half hours for the passers-by, police officers, tow truck drivers, and firefighters—about twenty-five people in all—to secure the car and pull the woman to safety.

All through the episode, the woman continued talking, repeating a phrase over and over to the rescuers. "It was kind'a funny," the fire captain recalled later. "She kept saying: 'I'll do it myself.'"

Fortunately for the young woman, the rescuers didn't listen to her. She survived the crash.

PARTNERSHIP MAY FEEL LEAST COMFORTABLE
WHEN IT IS MOST NECESSARY.

*It is amazing
what can be done if no one minds
who gets the credit.*

MARK TWAIN

*There are no
problems we cannot solve together,
and very few what we can
solve by ourselves.*

PRESIDENT LYNDON B. JOHNSON

It Isn't Good for Man to Live—
or Die—Alone

In the summer of 1995, the American Midwest experienced an oppressive heat wave. Day after day, the media announced the mounting number of people who had died because of the heat, particularly among the elderly. But there was one statistic that stands out in my mind. One newscaster reported that in the Chicago area alone, forty-one people died whose bodies remained unclaimed for days. Eventually, many of the bodies were taken by a friend or family member for burial, but some never were claimed.

No doubt some of those people didn't have any family in Chicago, but I believe many of them did. And that fact is really a commentary on the American population, which has become increasingly disenfranchised from any sense of community, intimacy, and commitment.

True, Americans have always celebrated rugged individualism. There is something in the American spirit that loves mavericks and renegades. But we seem to be growing even more detached from one another.

Yet the truth is, we need others—not only to perform better at work but to remain healthy emotionally, relationally, and spiritually. God was telling us something very important about ourselves when He said, "It isn't good for man to live alone." Our lives, our marriages, our work, and even our play are intended to be interdependent on others.

PARTNERSHIP IS A CRUCIAL PART
OF GOD'S DESIGN FOR US.

*It marks a big step
in your development when you realize
that other people can help you do a better job
than you could do alone.*

ANDREW CARNEGIE

We must all hang together,
else we shall all hang separately.

BENJAMIN FRANKLIN

(ON SIGNING THE DECLARATION OF
INDEPENDENCE)

PARTNERSHIPS WON'T WORK WITH JUST ...

A jawbone—

people who merely want to talk about it getting done,

a wishbone—

people who merely wish that someone would do it, or

a funnybone—

people who never get serious about getting it done.

Partnerships must have *a backbone*—

people who work together to get the job done.

A Natural Partnership

In 1961, Thomas van Beek, then a twenty-five year old executive, needed to hire a personal secretary. After a long and discouraging procession of unpromising applicants, a bright, charming young lady came into his office for an interview. Her name was Miss Neef. Her references were impeccable, her typing and shorthand were more than adequate, and more importantly, she projected an aura of personal stability, confidence, and energy. Tom hired her on the spot.

After Miss Neef's first week on the job, Tom was sure he had found the perfect assistant. She was an executive's dream. When she answered the phone, she projected authority; when faced with emergencies, she was always calm. She never seemed to grow weary or frayed from the stress.

Miss Neef was tireless. At the end of a long day—

even when her young employer was completely exhausted—she was always fresh and energetic. She never ceased to amaze him. He couldn't understand how she remained so energized, so on top of her game.

After twelve years, Tom discovered the answer to that mystery. Miss Neef told him she was ready to retire. She didn't desire another job offer, she was simply ready to step down as his private secretary.

Tom gracefully accepted her resignation and decided to throw her a going away party fitting for such a dedicated professional. He was going to do it up right.

He pulled out all the stops, and then he stopped dead in his tracks. For shortly after the guest of honor arrived—the guest of honor arrived. And the secret to Miss Neef's boundless energy was no longer a mystery. Where Tom had been certain for twelve years that his one secretary was doing the work of two, he discovered that *two* had been doing the work of one. Miss Neef was

actually two identical twin sisters sharing the same job. They had worked together so effectively and seamlessly that Tom never suspected. Each worked half the time and split the paycheck.

For more than a decade, the sisters worked in such a harmonious partnership—communicating, brain-storming, covering each other when needed—that no one knew, not even the person who spent forty hours a week with them. They were truly two working as one.

IN THE BEST PARTNERSHIPS,

TWO WORK AS ONE.

*I have long been profoundly
convinced that in the very nature of things,
employers and employees are partners,
not enemies; that their interests are common,
not opposed;
that in the long run the success
of each is dependent upon the success
of the other.*

JOHN D. ROCKEFELLER

FROM PERSECUTOR TO APOSTLE

Saul of Tarsus was a Pharisee's Pharisee. With a keen mind and absolute dedication to the Law, he made it his personal mission to track down and persecute Jews who followed "the Way" of Jesus Christ. But as every believer knows, Saul met Christ on the road to Damascus, and it changed his life. It even changed his name: from then on he became known as Paul.

His conversion caused such an uproar in Damascus that he had to escape secretly one night to avoid assassination. Paul decided to return to Jerusalem, but when he got there, he was shunned. His old colleagues rejected him—and his new Christian brothers didn't trust him. The memory of Paul encouraging the Jews to stone Stephen to death must have been too strong in their minds. Daily he tried to approach the disciples, but they would have nothing to do with him. He was an outcast.

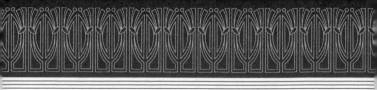

Then one day a man named Joseph approached Paul. He was one of the early leaders in the Jerusalem church. He took Paul in and insisted on personally escorting him to Peter, James, and the other elders in Jerusalem. When they doubted Paul's sincerity, Joseph defended him as a genuine disciple of Jesus, knowing Paul had preached Christ fearlessly in Damascus. Soon all of the believers welcomed him into their fellowship and ministry.

Paul was grateful to Joseph, who had a knack for seeing both the needs and the potential of the people he met. In fact, Joseph often reached out to underdogs. For that the apostles even gave him the nickname Barnabas, which means "son of encouragement." Maybe he did it because he had once been an underdog himself. It's said that Joseph was one of two men considered to replace Judas as the twelfth apostle, but when lots were cast, Matthias was chosen instead. Joseph never complained. He just kept on encouraging others.

In time, Paul and Joseph became close friends and ministry partners. Together they traveled far and wide, preaching the gospel. And Joseph didn't even mind when Paul passed him by and became his leader. Who was in charge wasn't important. What mattered was the partnership—and their ability to do great things together for God.

THE PERSON YOU HELP

MAY BECOME YOUR GREATEST

PARTNER.

Partnership Passage

"Heavenly Father...
I pray for them.
I'm not praying for the God-rejecting world
But for those you gave me, for they are yours by right.
Everything mine is yours, and yours mine.
And my life is on display in them.
For I'm no longer going to be visible in the world;
They'll continue in the world while I return to you.
Holy Father, guard them as they pursue this life
That you conferred as a gift through me,
So they can be one heart and mind
As we are one heart and mind."

John 17:9–11

Partnership Principles

Jesus considers us partners,
and prays for our welfare.

Jesus models that partners share in everything.

Jesus desires the best for his partners,
even when He is not with them.

Jesus longs and prays for us
to experience the same unity among each other that
He experiences with His Heavenly Father.

*Jesus always viewed people
from the perspective not just of what they
were but of what they could become.*

JOHN YATES

*You cannot sink
someone else's end of the boat and
still keep your own afloat.*

CHARLES BROWER

What's Best for the Rest

As much as any team in professional sports, the Boston Celtics of the 1960s are known for teamwork. Coach Red Auerbach was instrumental in the formation of that team and its values. He said he paid his players more for what they could do to help the team win than for their individual statistics. Auerbach once told this story about former Boston Celtic Satch Sanders:

There was a time around his third or fourth year when Satch Sanders got to thinking that it might be nice to score a few points on his own. So without being too obvious, he began taking more shots. One night he scored fifteen points. Another night he managed to get eighteen. Meanwhile, no one said a word about it. Our policy was that the ball belonged to everyone; nobody had exclusive rights to it. If you thought you had a good shot, you were not only encouraged to take it, you were expected to take it.

Then, one night he scored around twenty points, and we lost. It bothered him all the way home. He thought about it long into the night, than came to the following conclusion: "All it takes to upset the balance of this beautiful machine of ours is one man crossing over into another man's specialty. So I decided that night that it was a much bigger claim to say that I was a member of the world champion team than it was to say I averaged thirty-five points a game."

Talk about a winning attitude! Satch epitomized the way we played the game in Boston.

The Celtics of that era won an incredible eleven NBA titles. They've been called the greatest dynasty in the history of professional sports. And the key to those ongoing victories is the power of partnership.

THE BEST PARTNERSHIPS
TEACH SERVANTHOOD AND SELFLESSNESS.

Josefina's Secret Weapon

The July 19, 1948 edition of Time magazine told the astounding story of Josefina Guerrero who was awarded the Medal of Freedom for her heroic partnership with the American government in the face of the harsh brutality of World War II. During the war Joey, as she was called, spied for the Allied forces in Manila.

Joey was young, pretty, and vivacious. Her husband was a wealthy medical student at Santo Tomas University. But after the Japanese invaded the Philippines, she joined her friends and together they helped internees and the U.S. prisoners of war—bringing them food, clothing, and medicine. She also carried valuable information back to the U.S. military. She mapped the waterfront areas for the Allied army and prowled the restricted areas recording what she saw. From Joey's drawings, American planes were able to pinpoint their targets. She quickly won the respect and the appreciation of the U.S. officials.

For three years—until the war was over—Joey continued her cloak and dagger career—and was never caught. Sure, she was stopped several times by suspicious Japanese, but she was never captured or searched—due to her secret weapon. What was it? Leprosy!

As a leper she had been an outcast. No one wanted to have anything to do with her. After the war began, the very characteristic that had isolated her from others helped her to accomplish her mission. Her weakness became the secret of her strength.

God can do the same thing with our lives, individually and in partnership, to accomplish great things for His kingdom.

EVERY PERSON HAS THE POTENTIAL
TO ADD GREAT VALUE TO A PARTNERSHIP.

A Wink and a Smile

Who's the greatest college basketball coach of all time? Undoubtedly it's John Wooden. He coached the UCLA Bruins to more college basketball championships than any other NCAA coach in history. What was his secret to success? Teamwork. Not just the "Come one guys, let's all work together like a team" kind of thing while every player really does his own thing. Wooden produced the genuine article.

Coach Wooden insisted on a level of dedication and selflessness that is almost unheard of today. The team members all wore the same uniforms, the same kind of shoes—they were even instructed to put on their socks a particular way to protect their feet. And in the interest of uniformity, no player was allowed to sport facial hair. When a young recruit named Bill Walton was confronted with that rule, he said to Wooden, "Coach, I have a beard and I'm going to keep it."

Wooden simply smiled and said, "We're going to miss you, Bill." Needless to say, Walton shaved the beard.

Individual accomplishments and records held little value to Wooden. Every year he put together the best group of players he could find. And the five men who best complemented one another and worked together are the ones he started. But he didn't consider them to be any more important than the substitutes, his assistants, or even the equipment manager. His motto was, "The most important player when we win—is the rest of the team."

Wooden used to encourage his players to acknowledge the assists of their teammates. If one player received a pass that allowed him to score, Wooden wanted him to give the other man a wink or point to him as they moved down to the opposite end of the court.

"But what if the other player isn't looking when you point him out?" a new player asked Wooden once.

Wooden just smiled: "Oh, don't worry. He'll be looking." Coach Wooden understood people—and the power of partnership.

*The man who puts the
ball through the hoop has ten hands.*

JOHN WOODEN

*No one can whistle a symphony.
It takes an orchestra to play it.*

HAFFORD E. LUCCOCK

*Our world has become a neighborhood
without becoming a brotherhood.*

BILLY GRAHAM

*The most important
measurement of how good a game
I played was how much better I'd made
my teammates play.*

BILL RUSSELL

HE COULD DO NOTHING LESS

What would you have done if you'd been Abraham? When he was seventy-five years old, God told Abraham he would have a son. God promised that Abraham's name would be great and all the families of the earth would be blessed through him. In other words, God was choosing Abraham to be His partner.

But Abraham had to wait twenty-five years for that son to be born. He and his wife had long passed child-bearing age, yet God was true to His word and Isaac was born as Abraham approached age 100.

Isaac was the joy and delight of his parents. So imagine how Abraham felt when God asked him to do the unthinkable—to take the boy to a faraway mountain and offer him up as a sacrifice.

What Abraham couldn't know back then as he

traveled obediently toward the mountain was that God was doing something far bigger than what was affecting Abraham's small family. When Abraham told Isaac, "God will provide the lamb," his words applied not only to the circumstances that day but also to the salvation of mankind. As a covenant partner, God wouldn't ask Abraham to do something He wasn't prepared to do Himself. God spared Isaac that day, but when the time came 2000 years later, He gave His own Son so that we might live. And for that, we can all be eternally grateful.

THERE IS NO GREATER PARTNER
THAN GOD.